No One Told the Aardvark

Deborah Eaton and Susan Halter

Illustrated by Jim Spence

ini Charlesbridge

Sometimes I think it would be more fun to be an animal.
Today, at breakfast, I wanted to be a chimpanzee.
My dad said, "Please don't eat with your fingers. Use a spoon."

Chimpanzees don't have to use spoons.
They eat with their fingers **and** *their toes.*

When it was time for school, my big brother said,
"Tie your shoelaces. Let's get going."

Horses don't have to tie their shoelaces.
Their shoes are nailed on.

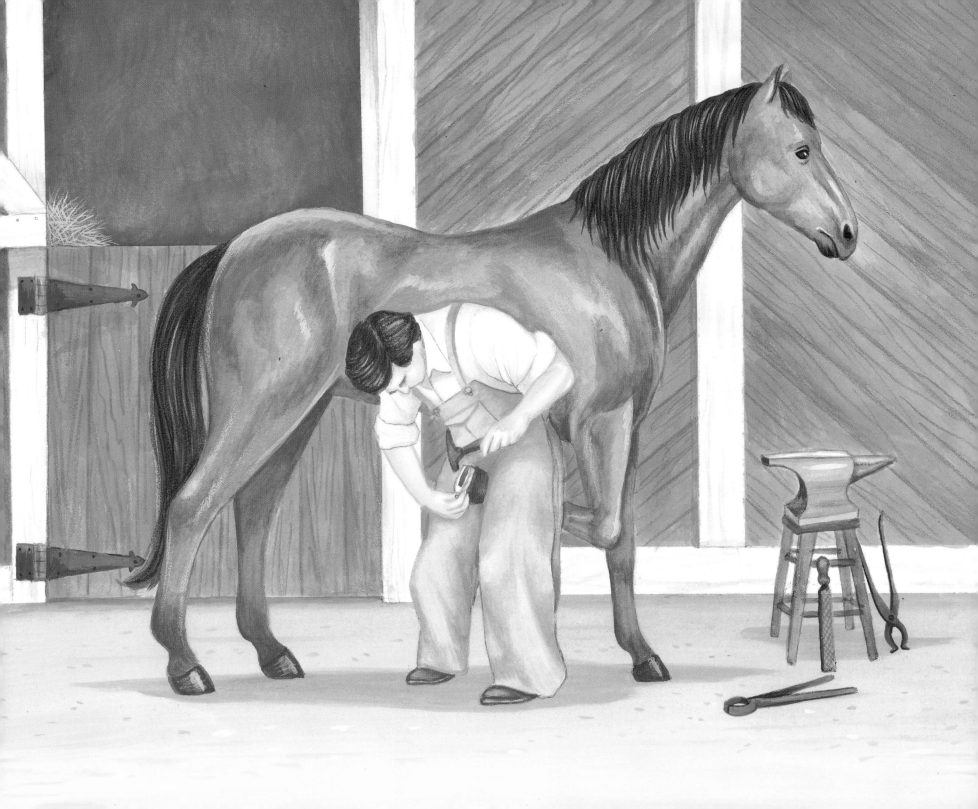

My friends yelled,
"Hurry up! Don't be so slow!"

Snails never have to hurry. It can take a snail three hours to crawl across a street.

At the corner, the crossing guard stopped me.
"Look both ways before you cross the street," he said.

Fish don't have to stop and look. My angelfish can look to the left and right at the same time.

At lunch, I remembered my mom telling me to "take small bites and chew my food."

Boa constrictors don't have to chew their food.
They swallow it in one piece.

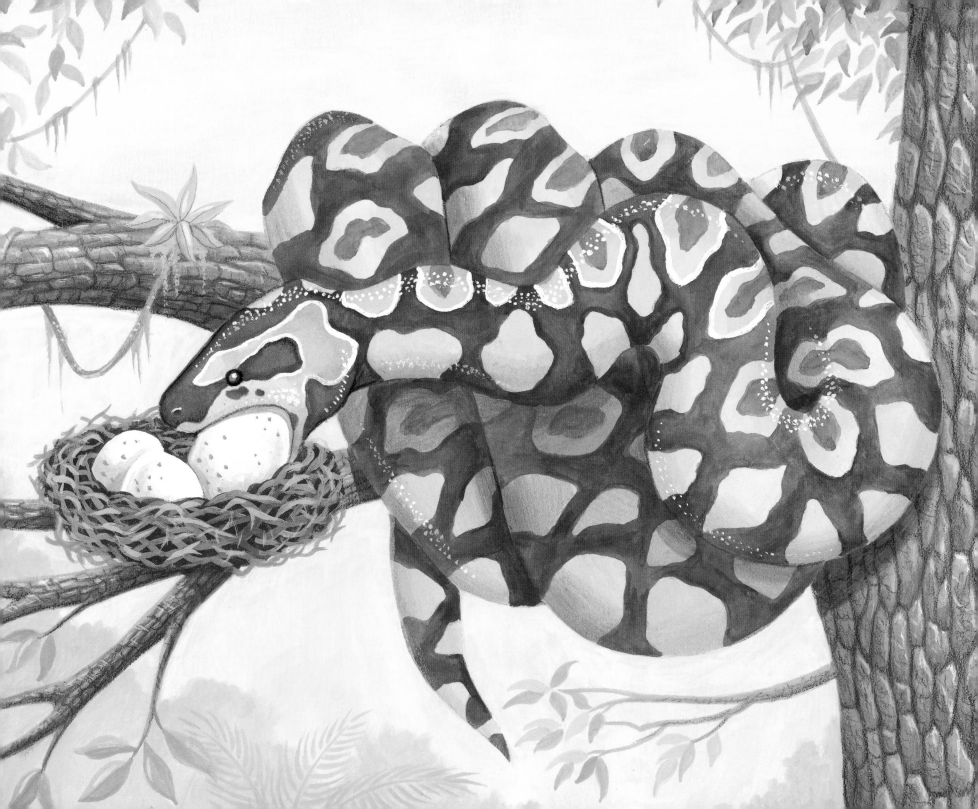

On our class trip to the zoo, I wanted to see the kangaroos.
But my teacher said, "Everyone stay together. Don't get lost."

*Baby kangaroos never get lost. They ride
inside their mothers' pouches.*

My little sister and I were playing after school.
"Hey!" she yelled. "It's not polite to stick out your tongue!"

*I guess no one told the aardvark. It sticks out its
tongue twelve whole inches to eat termites.*

My grampa stopped by before dinner, and when he saw my bedroom, he said, "Clean up that room, young man. It's a mess!"

Hermit crabs don't have to clean their rooms.
They just find new homes.

At dinner my aunt said, "If you want dessert,
first eat up all your vegetables!"

I told her baby blue whales don't eat vegetables. Instead,
they drink almost a hundred quarts of milk a day.

When I was taking my bath, my mom told me,
"Don't forget to wash behind your ears."

African elephants don't have to wash behind their ears.
They take dirt showers.

Then my big sister said,
"Brush your teeth before you go to bed."

I heard that Nile crocodiles never brush.
Tiny plovers pick their teeth clean.

It was getting dark. My gramma said,
"It's time to go to sleep, dear."

Raccoons don't have to go to sleep when it's dark.
They stay awake all night long.

Sometimes . . .

Sometimes I wish I were an animal—an elephant, a fish, a crab, or a raccoon, a kangaroo, a horse, or a whale, a snake, a crocodile, or a snail, an aardvark or a chimpanzee.

. . . . I wonder sometimes if they wish they were me.

Chimpanzee

Chimpanzees use their hands and feet to eat fruit, leaves, buds, bark, and insects. Chimpanzees may be messy eaters, but they have good manners when it comes to sharing their food with other chimps and cleaning each other's fur after meals.

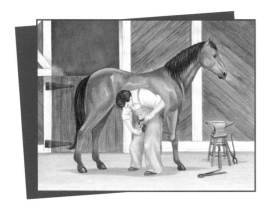

Horse

A horse's shoes are nailed onto its feet. The nails do not hurt because they go into a hard outer hoof. The hoof has to be trimmed regularly, just like your toenails do. Under the hoof, the horse has just one big toe.

Snail

A snail crawls by moving the muscles on its belly in waves. This isn't easy, so the snail lays down a slimy path to help it slide along smoothly. Tiny black eyes on the tips of its tentacles help it see where to go.

Angelfish

Angelfish have "all-around" vision. Each eye can move in a different direction so that one eye can look forward and the other can look backward at the same time. Instead of having to look for cars coming, angelfish watch out for big fish that might want to eat them. Even when they sleep, their eyes are open because, like all fish, they have no eyelids.

Boa Constrictor

A boa constrictor separates its upper jaw from its lower jaw in order to swallow food wider than its own mouth. After a big meal, a boa does not need to eat again for several months.

Kangaroo

A baby kangaroo, called a joey, stays safely tucked in its mother's pouch for about eight months. Even if the joey leaves the pouch, it jumps back in when it's time to go. This is a good thing, too, because its mother goes fast. The mother's hops are twenty feet long, and she can travel thirty-five miles per hour!

Aardvark

The aardvark sticks its snout into termite mounds to collect termites on its long, sticky tongue. An aardvark's snout is perfect for sniffing out termites, and thick nostril hair stops any termites from crawling into its nose! Its strong claws can rip a hole in a termite mound that's as hard as cement.

Hermit Crab

A hermit crab finds an empty snail shell to live in. It curls its long, soft body into the coils of the shell and doesn't come out until it needs a bigger home. When a hermit crab grows, it moves into a bigger shell from a periwinkle, whelk, or moon snail.

Blue Whale

Baby blue whales grow up to be the biggest animal on earth! Larger than the biggest dinosaur, blue whales can weigh up to two hundred tons. A blue whale calf gains almost ten pounds an hour, doubling in weight after just one week of drinking its mother's milk.

Elephant

Elephants like to cool off in water because the hot sun dries their skin. Afterward, they suck up dirt with their trunks and blow it over their wet bodies. This dust shower protects their skin from biting insects and sunburn.

Crocodile

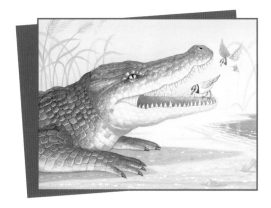

Crocodiles get their teeth cleaned by cooperative plovers. Plovers pick insects and leeches from crocodiles' mouths so well, you will probably never see a crocodile with cavities! Some plovers also act like washcloths and eat the ticks that get between crocodiles' scales.

Raccoon

Wide awake and hungry, raccoons prowl the night in search of food. They are omnivorous. Do you know what that means? It means they eat plants and animals, including grapes and corn, and crayfish, field mice, and crickets.

For Dona. It's the thought that counts.
—D. E.

To Bryan. Mom says, "I love you."
—S. H.

To my little girl, Sonnie
—J. S.

Published by Charlesbridge Publishing
85 Main Street, Watertown, MA 02472
(617) 926-0329
www.charlesbridge.com

Library of Congress Cataloging-in-Publication Data
Eaton, Deborah.
No one told the aardvark/by Deborah Eaton
and Susan Halter; illustrated by Jim Spence.
p. cm.
Summary: Compares children's expected behavior, such as washing behind their ears and
brushing their teeth, with the way animals conduct themselves to achieve the same result.
ISBN 0-88106-872-1 (reinforced for library use)
ISBN 0-88106-871-3 (softcover)
1. Animal behavior—Miscellanea—Juvenile literature.
2. Animals—Miscellanea—Juvenile literature.
[1. Animals—Habits and behavior—Miscellanea.]
I. Halter, Susan. II. Spence, Jim, ill. III. Title.
QL751.5.E245   1997
591—dc20   95-20078

Printed in the United States of America
(hc) 10 9 8 7 6 5 4 3 2 1
(sc) 10 9 8 7 6 5 4 3 2

The illustrations in this book were done in watercolors and colored pencil on illustration board.
The display type and text type were set in Korinna and Jokerman by Diane M. Earley.
Color separations were made by Pure Imaging, Watertown, Massachusetts.
Printed and bound by Worzalla Publishing Company, Stevens Point, Wisconsin
Production supervision by Brian G. Walker
Designed by Diane M. Earley